THE BUILD A BAG BOOK

Occasion Bags

Sew 15 stunning projects and endless variations

For those of you who can't have enough bags, in every colour and style for any occasion! For those who like to make a statement, be different, unique and classy. Enjoy!

DEDICATION

THE BUILD A BAG BOOK

Occasion Bags

Debbie Shore

SEARCH PRESS

First published in 2024

Search Press Limited
Wellwood, North Farm Road,
Tunbridge Wells, Kent TN2 3DR

Previously published as a hardback folder edition in 2018

Illustrations and text copyright © Debbie Shore 2024

Photographs copyright © Garie Hind 2024

Design copyright © Search Press Ltd. 2024

ISBN: 978-1-80092-110-8

Suppliers
If you have difficulty in obtaining any of the materials and equipment mentioned in this book, then please visit the Search Press website for details of suppliers:
www.searchpress.com

For further inspiration:

– join the Half Yard Sewing Club:
www.halfyardsewingclub.com

– visit Debbie's YouTube channel:
www.youtube.com/user/thimblelane

– visit Debbie's website: www.debbieshoresewing.com

Extra copies of the templates are available to download free from the Bookmarked Hub. Search for this book by title or ISBN: the files can be found under 'Book Extras'. Membership of the Bookmarked online community is free: www.bookmarkedhub.com

This is for Mum, not for encouraging me to sew, but for passing on her drawing and mathematical skills, both of which help when designing bags!

ACKNOWLEDGEMENTS

MIX
Paper | Supporting responsible forestry
FSC® C012521
FSC
www.fsc.org

CONTENTS

INTRODUCTION

Are you after a stylish new clutch or occasion bag? This book will help you create exactly what you're after. Using the two plastic templates provided you can create the 15 bag designs I've included, but you can then use the templates over and over again to mix and match the different shapes of flaps and have fun with colours and textures of fabric to create your own unique designs.

The templates included will allow you to make a handbag with sides and base, a pouch and a clutch bag, each with three distinctive styles of flap: round, curved or scalloped. Choose either a long, wide strap or a narrow wristlet, then add patch or zipped pockets to the lining or outside of your bag. Simply draw around your chosen template onto fabric and cut, with no need for pins! The templates are semi-transparent to enable fussy cutting, and are easy to store and wipe clean. Extra hardware can be added to give a shop-bought look to your handbag, including metal closures, D-rings and swivel snaps – I've included instructions on fitting the most popular styles.

Use a 5mm (¼in) seam allowance unless otherwise stated – this is included in your template measurements. Each bag will require approximately 66 x 51cm (26 x 20in) outer fabric for the bag, 61 x 33cm (24 x 13in) contrast fabric for the flap and strap, 66 x 51cm (26 x 20in) lining fabric and 66 x 51cm (26 x 20in) fusible fleece or interfacing, plus any extra fabric for trimmings and pockets. Enjoy!

See pages 38–43.

See pages 68–71.

See pages 28–33.

This fringed handbag with knotted strap is a stylish option for a night out. The curved flap fastens with a magnetic snap fastener for a bit of extra security. See pages 64–67.

UNDERSTANDING THE TEMPLATES

Your templates are semi-transparent so that you can place them over a particular area of your fabric to fussy cut a pattern if you wish; they are also wipe-clean and easy to store flat. Use an erasable ink pen or chalk pencil to draw your chosen outline.

SELECTING THE TEMPLATES

Whenever you need to use a template, your project instructions will clearly tell you which one to use, and show the template with the relevant parts highlighted (as shown here – here you can see the templates required are the occasion bag outline from template 1 and the bag base from template 2). Some of the pieces will need to be cut on the fold of the fabric, so you will need to place your template on the fold where indicated, as shown below.

Template 1

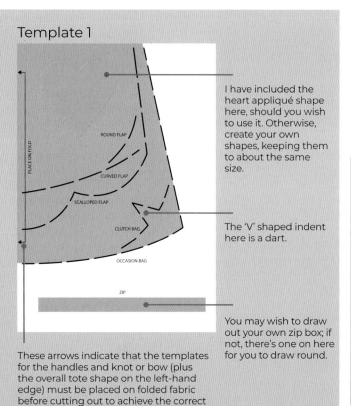

I have included the heart appliqué shape here, should you wish to use it. Otherwise, create your own shapes, keeping them to about the same size.

The 'V' shaped indent here is a dart.

You may wish to draw out your own zip box; if not, there's one on here for you to draw round.

These arrows indicate that the templates for the handles and knot or bow (plus the overall tote shape on the left-hand edge) must be placed on folded fabric before cutting out to achieve the correct dimensions, unless specified otherwise. Align the indicated edge with the fold of the fabric.

Template 2

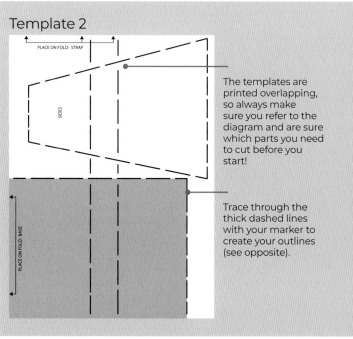

The templates are printed overlapping, so always make sure you refer to the diagram and are sure which parts you need to cut before you start!

Trace through the thick dashed lines with your marker to create your outlines (see opposite).

USING THE TEMPLATES

1 Refer to the pattern pieces needed for each style of bag. Where indicated, place the template over the fold of your fabric.

2 Then simply draw through the slots in your template to mark the outline of your bag pieces.

3 Make sure you draw, then cut out the 'V' shapes in the curve of the clutch bag – these are darts – which when sewn together will give your bag shape.

4 Cut out as many pieces as required, by following the drawn dashed lines.

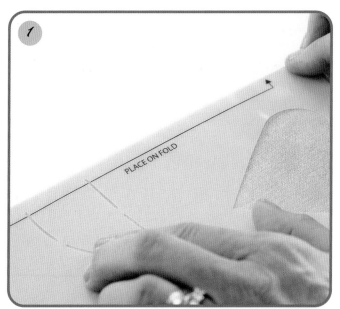

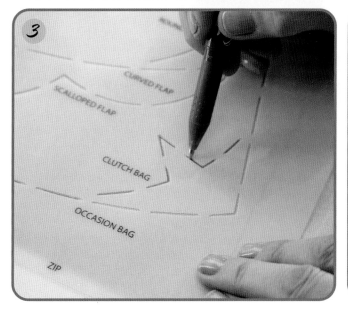

This patchworked and quilted clutch is a great way of using up small scraps of treasured fabrics, while the wristlet and magnetic snap fastener make it practical for carrying around town. See pages 68–71.

Featuring piping and a tongue clasp, this sophisticated bag is practical and hardwearing, as it features a mesh bag base. See pages 72–75.

MATERIALS

1. FABRICS

When I'm sewing bags, I choose the colour and pattern of fabric I like, then worry about the fibre content later. The perfect weight for a bag is upholstery fabric – the kind you'd use for curtains – a heavy woven cotton that is durable but is still easy to sew. However, **cotton (1a)** is a favourite of mine. If it is too lightweight, add fusible fleece or interfacing to the wrong side to add rigidity (see opposite). This is imperative if you're using stretch fabric, as you don't want a bouncy bag!

If you want to try out other fabrics, **satin (1b)** makes a beautifully elegant evening clutch but can be difficult to sew as it tends to fray. If you like this look, consider choosing a satin polyester instead of silk – it's easier to work with and more affordable too! Alternatively, create a casual look with corduroy or **denim (1c)** or both!

If you choose **laminated fabric (1d)**, a non-stick presser foot for your machine will help to feed the coated fabric through easily.

I don't pre-wash fabric for bag making as it's unlikely to need laundering, and I like the starchy, crisp feel of new fabrics. Most bags can be spot-cleaned, but spray them with fabric protector if you wish, to guard against stains.

1a

1b

1c

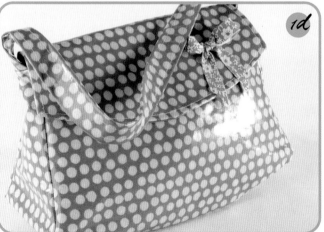

1d

2. FABRIC SUPPORTS

Most of the fabrics I use for bag making need a little support to give them rigidity and form. I generally use **fusible fleece**, which is a 3mm ($\frac{1}{8}$in) thick polyester padding with adhesive dots on one side that fuse the fleece to the wrong side of the fabric when ironed. (Refer to the manufacturer's instructions, as some need steam and some don't.)

Interfacing (2a) is either woven or non-woven iron-on stabilizer, available in different weights, from a fine sheet that can prevent knit fabrics from stretching or loose-weave fabrics from twisting, to a leather-like material that will produce quite a stiff bag. I would avoid the latter if you are a new sewer, as it can be quite difficult to work with. Experiment with different weights of interfacings: if you buy from a shop, you will have an idea of how firm your fabric will be when you feel the interfacing and see how it drapes.

Wadding or batting (2b) (same thing!) can also be used to give a softer feel to your bag, and is available in a wide range of natural and man-made fibres. Use spray fabric adhesive if you wish to secure it to the back of your fabric before sewing.

Foam stabilizer is an excellent choice for larger bags; this is a 5mm ($\frac{1}{4}$in) thick foam that will allow your bag to stand up unaided. Buy either sew-in or single-sided fusible versions. I haven't used it in any of the projects here, but it might be something you want to experiment with. Trim it back to the seams to make it easier to sew.

For most of the projects in this book I've kept things simple by using fusible fleece throughout, whether I've used upholstery fabric or craft cotton to create my bags. The exception is laminated fabric or faux leather, which can't be ironed from the right side. In these cases I adhere the fleece with repositionable spray fabric adhesive.

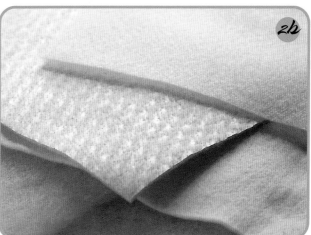

3. THREADS

It's important to use good-quality thread when making bags to achieve the strongest seams. After all, when you've gone to the expense of buying beautiful fabric and spent your precious time making a bag, you don't want your seams to let you down! A quality thread will be smooth and not fibrous; don't use old or inexpensive thread. If in doubt, do the tug test: if you yank the thread from the spool and it snaps, it's also likely to snap when sewing.

TOOLS

1. SEWING MACHINE

Although you'll mainly be using a straight stitch, your bag fabric could be quite heavy, so you may need a machine that has the power to push the needle through the material. I'd always recommend a computerized machine as they are feature-packed and easy to use; choose a big brand that comes with a warranty and customer support. Buy a few denim needles, too – these are strong needles that will easily slip through thick or tough fabrics.

2. PRESSER FEET

Your machine will have standard, buttonhole and zipper feet for most of your sewing needs, but it is worth investing in a walking foot to help sew through multiple layers of fabrics to prevent them slipping, a darning foot (shown) for free-motion embroidery, and a non-stick foot for laminated fabrics.

3. SHEARS

Dressmaking shears with angled handles make cutting straight lines and multiple layers a breeze.

4. SMALL SCISSORS

Embroidery scissors are useful for snipping small threads and buttonholes.

5. PINKING SHEARS

The serrated blades on pinking shears cut at small 45-degree angles to prevent woven fabric from fraying. They are a terrific way of finishing seams and also useful for cutting quickly into curved areas, such as bag flaps.

6. ROTARY CUTTER, RULER AND CUTTING MAT

These three tools go hand in hand to make light work of cutting accurately. Choose the largest self-healing mat you have room for. A 45mm ($1\frac{3}{4}$in) rotary cutter is the most used but a 60mm ($2\frac{3}{8}$in) makes it easier to cut through multiple layers of fabric and wadding/batting. A 61cm (24in) rectangular ruler with 45-degree markings is also useful for cutting on the bias.

7. TAILOR'S HAM

These are sawdust-filled shapes that are pushed inside your bag to enable you to press the seams without pressing your bag flat, while also keeping your hands out of the way of a hot iron!

8. MARKING TOOLS

To draw around your templates you'll need some form of marking pen. I use erasable ink pens, whereby the ink disappears using the heat of an iron or with water, or fades away over the course of a few hours. Beware of ironing over water- or air-erasable ink, as the heat can make the ink permanent! I would advise you only use the heat-erasable pens in the seam allowances, as they may mark your fabric. Fabric or chalk pencils are also a good option – simply brush away the markings when they're not needed any more.

9. ADHESIVES

A tacking/basting glue stick offers a quick way of holding seams together before sewing; I use this to secure zips instead of hand-tacking/basting to save time. Repositionable spray fabric adhesives are an excellent choice for bonding wadding/batting to the wrong side of fabrics. Permanent adhesives in wet glue form are strong enough to secure embellishments to your bag, while spray adhesives make light work of appliqué.

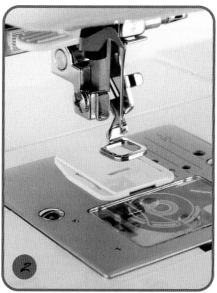

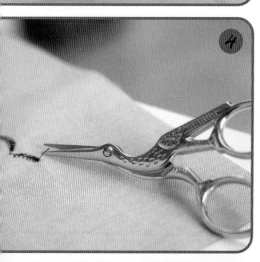

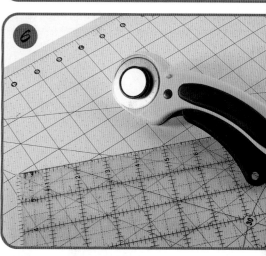

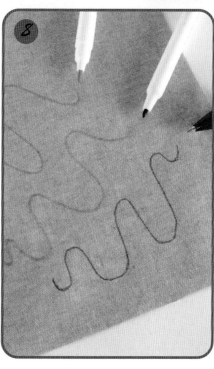

HARDWARE

Shop-bought handles, metal fasteners and rings are the touches that give your bag or purse a professional finish (see top right). Shop around for bag feet, zip ends, swivel snaps and metal rings to attach straps. If you can't find anything, a good place to look is your local charity or thrift shop, where you could find amazing hardware on used, affordable bags that can be taken apart and recycled.

Cotton webbing (below right) is useful for making shoulder straps, and is available in a rainbow of colours. The ends tend to fray easily, so to stop this, either seal the ends with heat from a flame, or sew a zigzag stitch over them.

An easy way to brighten up your bag would be to add a colourful button (see below) – either as a decorative element or practical – while buckles aren't just for fastening straps: some are quite decorative and make unusual embellishments. The chain strap clutch on page 84 shows how the right button can transform a bag and add real impact.

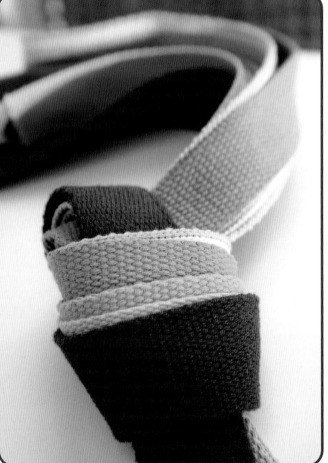

TECHNIQUES

FABRIC FLOWER

This pretty rose-like flower adds a personal touch to the flap of a bag – try adding a brooch pin to the back to make it removable.

1 Cut a length of fabric measuring 51 x 6.5cm (20 x 2½in). Fold it in half lengthways, right sides together, then cut the ends in a curve towards the fold, as shown. Sew the raw edges together, leaving a turning gap in the centre of the seam of about 10cm (4in). Trim with pinking shears.

2 Turn right side out and press. Begin to roll the strip from one end, adding a small spot of glue at every turn to secure.

3 After every couple of turns, twist the fabric over: this will create the petal effect.

4 When you come to the end of the fabric strip, add one final spot of glue and leave to dry. Either sew or glue onto your bag to finish.

FREE-MOTION EMBROIDERY

Think of your needle and thread as a pen and ink, but instead of moving the pen over the paper, you move the fabric under the needle to create your own unique designs. Your sewing machine will need two things: first, a drop-feed-dog facility. The feed dogs are the teeth that carry the fabric through the machine and by dropping these out of the way, or covering them over, you have control of moving the fabric in any direction you like. The second thing you need is a free-motion or darning foot. This foot 'hops' across the fabric and allows you to see where you're stitching. It's a good idea to practise on a piece of fabric you're not too precious about, so get your machine set up and have a play.

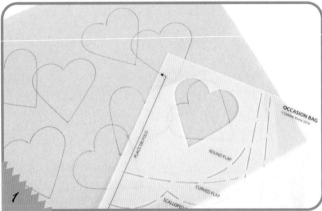

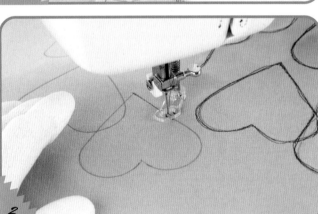

1 Draw your design in erasable ink (or you could embroider around the edge of the pattern of the fabric).

2 Pop your fabric under the needle, put your foot on the pedal and start to sew. Lay your hands flat either side of the needle, and move the fabric from side to side, up and down, around in circles, creating swirls and zigzags – move the fabric any way you wish and keep it moving! You may like to invest in quilters' gloves; these help your fingers to 'grip' the fabric.

3 It's good practice to stop after the first few stitches, leaving the needle down, and snip off the excess thread so you don't sew over it. You'll realize as you're sewing that the faster you move the fabric, the longer the stitch. There are no rules – simply stitch at a speed you feel comfortable with and that produces a stitch you like the look of.

4 It's also a great way of sewing on appliqué!

FABRIC STRAPS

There are two types of fabric strap for you to make in this book: open-ended and closed-ended. The open-ended straps are sewn into the top seams of your bag; the closed-ended ones are sewn to the front of your bag.

Add interfacing or fusible fleece to the wrong side of your fabric strips if you need a stiffer handle, or give them a blast of spray starch for a crisp finish. You can make the straps shorter if needed just by cutting off some of the length, or extend the straps by elongating the template.

Open-ended strap

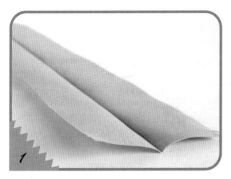 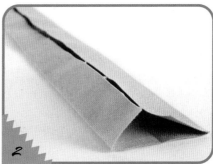 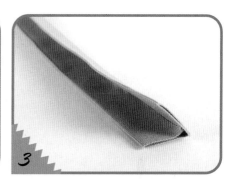

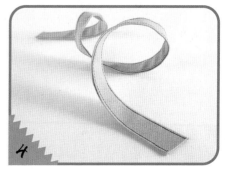

1 Cut out your fabric as per the instructions in your project, using the template. Fold the fabric in half lengthways and press.

2 Open out the fabric, fold the two long sides to the centre and press again.

3 Fold the whole strap in half again and press.

4 Top-stitch along both long sides of your strap to complete. Your strap is now ready to insert into the seams of your bag.

Closed-ended strap

Follow steps 1–3 as above.

4 Fold the long sides of the strap together so that the raw edges are on the outside. Sew across the bottom.

5 Turn right side out, then top-stitch all around the edge.

 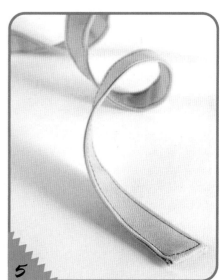

ZIPPED POCKET

I call this a 'letterbox' zip, as the opening reminds me of a letterbox and the lining fabric is 'posted' through the hole. I use it to create pockets in bag linings, and this is what I'm showing here, but you could also use this technique on the outer fabric of a bag. I prefer to use continuous zipping, as it can be cut to the size required.

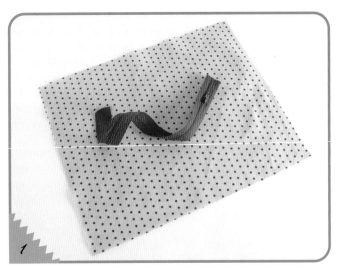

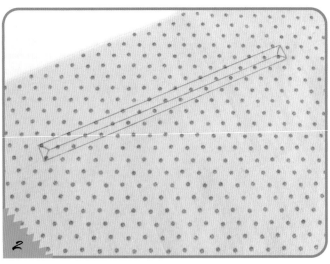

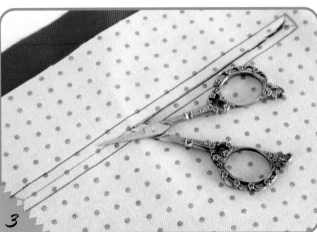

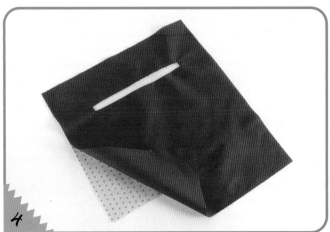

1 Cut two pieces of pocket lining fabric to the size of the pocket you need. This should be shorter than your bag lining fabric, and can either be the same width, so that the pocket is sewn into the side seam, or narrower than the bag. Choose a zip that is 2.5–5cm (1–2in) longer than the pocket opening – it will sit flatter when the ends (with the metal stoppers) are cut off. Alternatively, cut a length of continuous zipping to size.

2 Draw a rectangle onto the wrong side of one pocket lining piece in the position you'd like the zip, measuring 1cm (½in) wide, and the length of the zip opening. Draw another line straight through the centre of the box, with a 'Y' shape at each end going into the corners of the rectangle.

3 Pin this pocket piece right sides together to your bag lining fabric. With a small stitch on your machine, carefully sew around the box. Take a small, sharp pair of scissors and cut along the centre line, then into the 'Y' shape up to, but not through the stitches. Remove the pins.

4 Push the lining through the hole, and press.

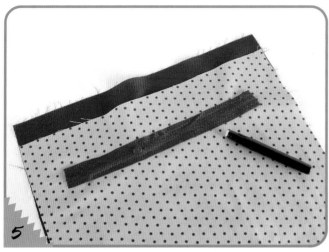

5

6a

6b

6c

5 Place the zip behind the hole with the teeth facing down, as shown. Either tack/baste or use a temporary glue stick to hold the zip in place. Sew around the edge of the zip on your machine; move the zip head out of the way as you sew round, to avoid wiggly stitch lines.

21

6 Pin the two pocket pieces right sides together, keeping the bag lining out of the way. If your pocket is going to fit into the side seam (as shown in steps 6a and 6b), sew across the top and bottom of the pocket. Then, tack/baste the pocket to the side of the lining. Remove the pins.

Alternatively, if your pocket is narrower than the width of the lining, sew all the way around the two pocket pieces, avoiding sewing through the bag lining fabric (6c).

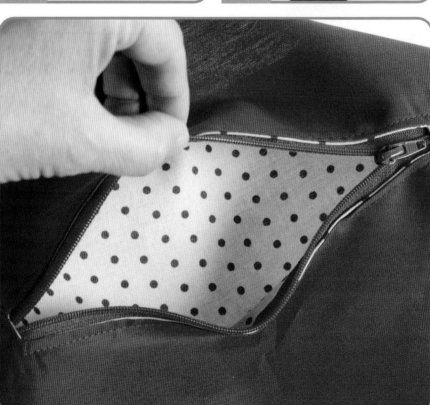

Finished zipped pocket.

PIPING

A strip of piping around a bag or across a pocket gives a professional finishing touch to your work, and is simple to make yourself. Cord comes in many assorted widths; I'd use a fine cord on pockets, and up to 5mm (¼in) wide cord for the bag seams.

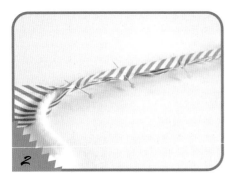
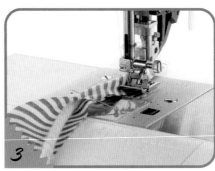
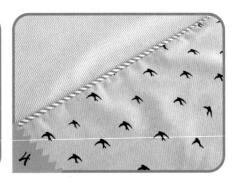

1 Cut your fabric into strips that are wide enough to wrap around the cord and go under the sewing machine needle. If you're taking the piping around corners and curves, cut the fabric strips on the bias; if your piping is sewn into a straight seam, as for the piped handbag on pages 72–75, then you can cut on the straight of grain.

2 Pin the raw edges together, wrong sides facing, sandwiching the cord in the centre.

3 With the zipper foot on your machine, sew alongside the cord, making sure the raw edges of the strip are together. Take out the pins as you sew.

4 To apply the piping, sandwich it between the two pieces of fabric, right sides and raw edges together, then sew with your zipper foot. (Piping feet are available for some sewing machines.) If you're a beginner, you may find it easier to sew the piping to one side of the fabric at a time.

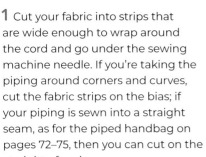

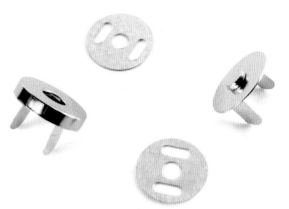

FUSSY CUTTING

This is a method of cutting out a particular part of the pattern on your fabric, for instance if you wanted to feature a specific part of the design on a pocket or flap. As your templates are semi-transparent, simply place them over the area you wish to cut, trace around the pattern and cut out!

MAGNETIC SNAP FASTENERS

These simple-to-fit clasps don't usually come with instructions, so this is how to fit them. I'd recommend placing a scrap of fabric behind the clasp, on the wrong side of your fabric, to stabilize the fabric and help to stop the clasps pulling. The clasps come in two parts with a disc-shaped back section for each side. If you're fitting to a bag with a flap, the narrower part of the clasp will go onto the flap and the wider section onto the bag.

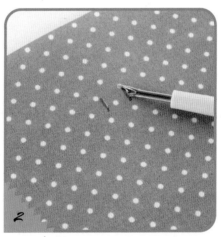

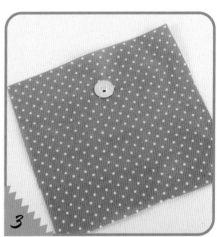

1 Mark the position of the clasp with an erasable ink pen, by taking the back of the clasp and drawing through the hole in the centre, then mark the two long holes either side.

2 Take your seam ripper or a small pair of sharp scissors, and make a small incision over the long lines. It's better to make the cuts too small so they can be made bigger; if you cut them too big, you may ruin your project.

3 Push the prongs of the clasps through the holes and then through the slots on the backing plates.

4 Open out the prongs on the back of the fabric. It doesn't really matter whether you open them outwards or close them inwards, but I find them easier to open outwards as shown.

DEBBIE'S TOP TIPS

1 Start with a simple project such as the zip clutch (see right and pages 56–59). As your skills grow you'll be adding piping, pockets and hardware in no time!

2 Make up your bag in an inexpensive fabric like calico first: that way, if things go wrong, you're not wasting anything but your time. You may even like your calico version!

3 Always start and stop your stitching with a couple of backstitches to prevent the thread unravelling. Some machines have a lock/fix stitch that puts four stitches on top of each other to do the same job.

4 When sewing in the base of a bag, match the end of the base panel to the edge of the bottom of the bag fabric, so you start sewing 5mm (¼in) from each edge.

5 Cut your fabric pieces on the grain – this means that the weave of the fabric sits vertically and horizontally. If you cut at an angle (on the bias), your fabric could twist.

6 To help you sew in a straight line with even seam allowances, place a strip of masking tape over the bed of your sewing machine as a guide for your fabric; measure from the needle 5mm (¼in) to the right and place your tape at this point (see right). An elastic band around the free arm works well too.

7 Top-stitching can be a bit daunting, so sew slowly and use a thread that matches your fabric if you're not very confident. Remember, a decorative button is an effective way of hiding wobbly stitches!

8 Pin at right angles to the edge of your fabric. You'll find the layers don't slip, and although you should be taking out your pins as you sew, if the needle accidentally hits a pin, there is less chance of either breaking (see right).

9 Change your sewing machine needle regularly – it is recommended you put a new needle in after every eight hours of sewing. You'll notice a difference to the stitches and even the sound of your machine! It's always good form when you change the needle to take off the needle plate and clear out any lint. Refer to your sewing machine manual.

10 Relax! Sewing is fun! Don't worry if things go a bit wrong. Put your work down and come back to it the next day – it won't seem half as bad as you thought!

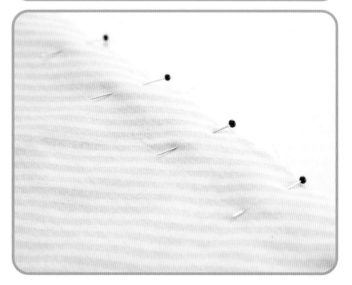

GLOSSARY

Edge stitch:
Stitching close to the edge of your work, for instance around the top of a bag or flap.

Top-stitch:
Stitching on top of your work that can be seen, either decorative or purposeful, for instance around the top of a bag to neaten and hold the lining and outer pieces together.

Raw edge:
The unfinished edge of your fabric.

Right/wrong sides together:
The right side of your fabric is the side you want to be seen, the wrong side is the back of the fabric. When sewing two sections of your bag together, it's usually with two pieces of the same side facing.

Seam allowance:
The distance between your stitches and the edge of the fabric. I've used a 5mm (¼in) seam allowance for the projects in this book.

Back-tack:
Always start and end a row of stitches by sewing a couple of stitches backwards, as this prevents the stitches from coming undone.

Wadding/batting/fleece:
The fleecy layer between the lining and outer sections of the bag, giving it shape and rigidity (see page 13).

Trimmings:
Decorative elements such as the finishing on the fringed bag (see page 64) or the large button on the chain strap clutch (see page 84).

Appliqué:
Fabric shapes sewn to the bags as decoration, such as the heart on the slim bag (see page 76).

The Projects

CURVED FLAP HANDBAG

This gorgeous floral bag features softly feminine fabric. It's a fine dressmaking fabric, so I used fusible fleece on the wrong side to give it a bit more sturdiness. The green fabric is a linen-look cotton. To change the look you could swap in a different flap, add a thicker strap, take the strap into the side seams of the bag or choose different fastenings as you wish!

You will need

- 91.5 x 56cm (36 x 22in) patterned outer fabric for the bag
- 91.5 x 81.5cm (36 x 32in) contrast plain fabric for the flap, strap and lining
- 91.5 x 56cm (36 x 22in) fusible fleece or interfacing
- Magnetic snap fastener
- Two 13mm (½in) D-rings
- Two swivel snaps
- Wet fabric glue

Finished size

28 x 20.5 x 10cm (11 x 8 x 4in), excluding strap

Using your templates

You will need to use the occasion bag outline from TEMPLATE 1, the curved flap outline from TEMPLATE 1, the strap outline from TEMPLATE 2, the side panel from TEMPLATE 2 and the bag base from TEMPLATE 2. All templates except the bag side should be placed on the fold of the fabric as indicated.

Template 1

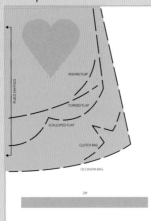

Template 1

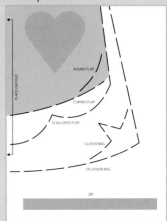

Template 2

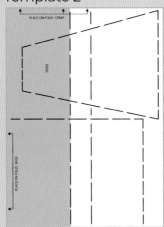

Template 2

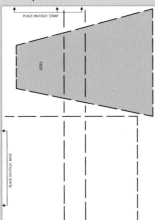

Template 2

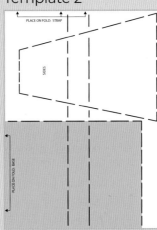

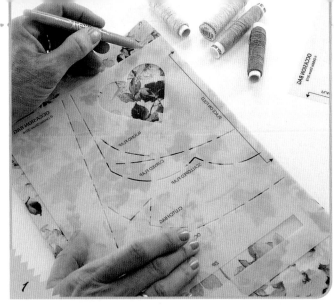

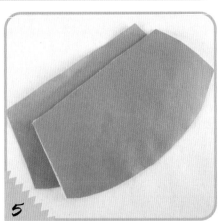

1 Fold your fabric in half, place the template over the fold as indicated, and draw around the occasion bag markings.

2 Cut two pieces from outer fabric and two from lining. Fuse fleece to the wrong sides of the outer pieces.

3 Cut two outer and two lining bag side pieces and, again, fuse fleece to the wrong sides of the outer pieces.

4 With your fabric on the fold, trace the outline of the bag base, then cut one from outer fabric and one from lining. Fuse fleece to the wrong side of the outer fabric.

5 Cut two curved flap pieces from lining fabric, then fuse fleece to the wrong side of one piece.

6 Fold the flap piece without fleece in half and crease to màrk the centre, then apply the slimmer part of the magnetic snap fastener as explained on page 23, 2.5cm (1in) from the curved edge.

7

8

9

10

11

7 Sew the two flap pieces right sides together, leaving the straight top edge open. Snip off the corners and trim the curved seam with pinking shears, then turn right side out and press.

8 Top-stitch around the seam.

9 Fix the second part of the magnetic snap fastener to the front of the bag, centrally, 7.5cm (3in) from the top.

10 Sew the side panels right sides together to the back of the bag.

11 Sew the final panel to the side seams to form a 'tube'. To make the seams crisp, press the seam with the wrong sides together, then top-stitch close to the edge (this is an optional step).

12

13

14

15

16

12 Pin the flap to the centre back of the bag, right sides together, then tack/baste across the top. Remove the pins.

13 Cut one piece of strap fabric using the template; adjust the length of the strap if you wish to make it longer or shorter. Make up a closed-ended strap following the instructions on page 19. Cut two 5cm (2in) lengths from the strap. Fold each through a D-ring and secure with a spot of glue. Hold in place with fabric clips. (Gluing simply helps to keep the ends of the straps together before sewing, but you can leave this stage out if you prefer.)

14 Tack/baste one tab to each side of the outer bag, facing downwards.

15 Sew the bag base in place, right sides together; start and stop your seams 5mm (¼in) from the corners. Turn right side out and press, then top-stitch around the seam if you wish.

16 Thread each end of the strap through a swivel snap, and sew.

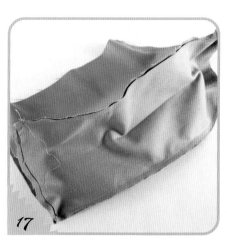

17

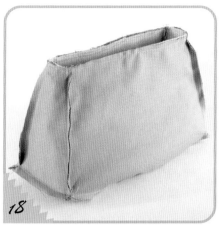

18

19

17 Sew the front, back, side and base lining pieces together in the same way as the outer bag, right sides facing, but this time leave a turning gap in one base seam of about 10cm (4in); it should be large enough to put your hand through.

18 Drop the outer bag inside the lining so that the right sides are together. Sew around the top, matching the side seams. You will find this easier if you use the free arm on your sewing machine.

19 Pull the lining through the turning gap, then sew the opening closed.

20 Push the lining inside the bag and press. Top-stitch around the top of the bag using the free arm on your machine.

21 Clip on the strap. Decorate with a handmade fabric rose: see page 17.

20

If you find top-stitching the seams difficult, leave this step out, or try using a hand-sewn blanket stitch for a rustic effect.

Tip

ROUND FLAP HANDBAG

When I cut out the flap for this handbag I thought it looked a little plain, so I decided to use one of the flowers from my patterned fabric and appliqué it in place. I then decided to use a magnetic snap for my fastening as it adds security but won't be seen, so won't spoil the clean look of the bag.

I've also added a letterbox zipped pocket to the inside (see pages 20–21). I've used craft cotton for this bag, while the outer fabric is backed with fusible fleece.

Using your templates

You will need to use the occasion bag outline from TEMPLATE 1, the round flap from TEMPLATE 1, the wide strap outline from TEMPLATE 2, the side panel from TEMPLATE 2 and the bag base from TEMPLATE 2. All templates except the bag side should be placed on the fold of the fabric as indicated.

Template 1

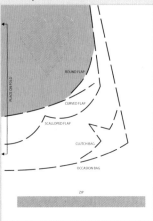

Template 1

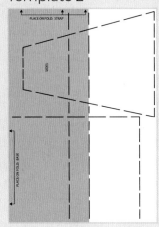

Template 2

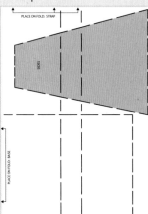

Template 2

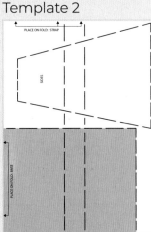

Template 2

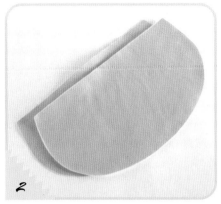

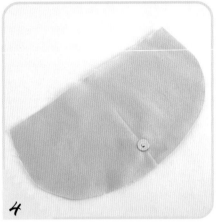

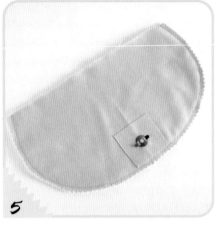

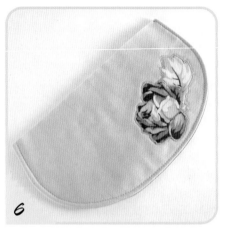

1 Fold your plain fabric in half and place the flap template over the fold, where instructed. Draw through the round flap markings.

2 Cut out two flap pieces of fabric and fuse fleece to the wrong side of one of them.

3 Cut out a flower shape from your patterned fabric and adhere it to the right side of the flap fabric backed with fleece, with either spray fabric glue or an adhesive sheet. Using a small, narrow zigzag stitch on your sewing machine, carefully sew around the edge of the appliqué.

4 Fix the narrower half of the magnetic snap fastener to the remaining flap fabric, centrally, 2.5cm (1in) from the curved edge.

5 Sew the two flap pieces right sides together, leaving the straight top side open. Snip around the curve with pinking shears.

6 Turn right side out and top-stitch around the curved seam.

7 Fold your outer and lining fabrics in half and draw around the occasion bag shape. Cut two from outer fabric and two from lining. Also cut two side panel pieces from outer fabric and two from lining. Fuse fleece to the wrong sides of the outer pieces. Fit the thicker part of the magnetic snap fastener centrally to the front panel, 7.5cm (3in) from the top.

8 Sew the side panels to the front and back of the bag, right sides together, then sew in the base. Turn right side out.

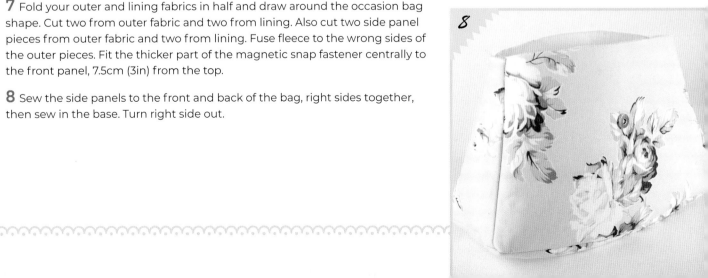

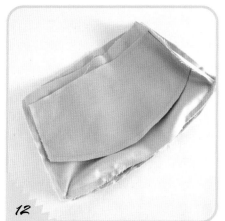

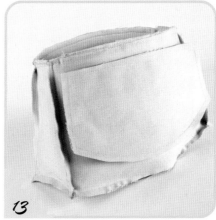

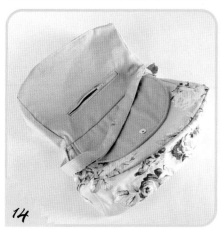

9 Pin the flap centrally to the back of the bag, right sides together. Tack/baste across the top. Remove the pins.

10 Cut a piece of strap fabric using the template; adjust the length of the strap if you wish to make it longer or shorter. Make up an open-ended strap following the instructions on page 19.

11 Tack/baste the strap facing downwards to each top side of the bag. Be careful to make sure the strap isn't twisted!

12 Add a letterbox zipped pocket to the lining if you wish, following the instructions on pages 20–21. Sew together the front and back pieces with the sides, then add the base, leaving a turning gap of about 10cm (4in) in one base seam.

13 Drop the outer bag inside the lining so the two are right sides together. Sew around the top, making sure the flap and straps are tucked away inside, and your seams match.

14 Turn right side out, then sew the opening closed.

15 Push the lining inside the bag and press, then top-stitch around the top edge to complete.

SCALLOPED FLAP HANDBAG

I've added an adjustable strap to this bag so that it can be worn either over the shoulder or across the body. The black and stone colour combination of print and plain fabrics give it a modern, edgy look. My plain fabric is linen, which you may prefer to back with stabilizer as it has quite a loose weave, and the print is a craft cotton.

Using your templates

Template 1

Template 1

Template 2
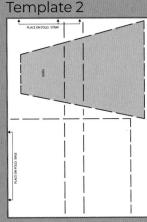

Template 2
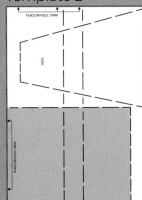

You will need

- 91.5 x 56cm (36 x 22in) patterned fabric
- 91.5 x 71cm (36 x 28in) plain fabric: I used the same fabric for the lining and flap
- 91.5 x 56cm (36 x 22in) fusible fleece
- 102cm (40in) of 2.5cm (1in) wide webbing
- Two 2.5cm (1in) rectangular rings
- 2.5cm (1in) slider
- 13 x 30.5cm (5 x 12in) bag base or firm stabilizer
- Strong wet fabric glue

Finished size

28 x 20.5 x 10cm (11 x 8 x 4in), excluding strap

You will need to use the occasion bag outline from TEMPLATE 1, the scalloped flap from TEMPLATE 1, the side panel outline from TEMPLATE 2 and the bag base from TEMPLATE 2. All templates except the bag side should be placed on the fold of the fabric as indicated.

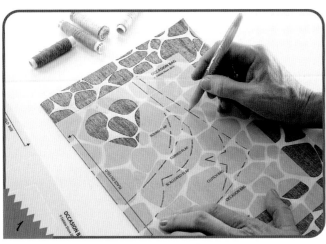

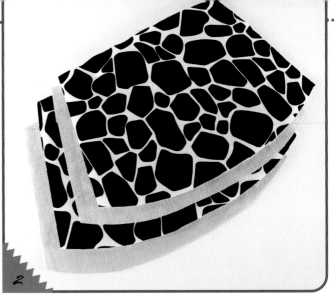

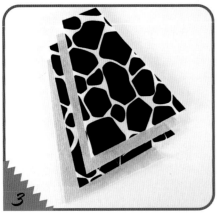

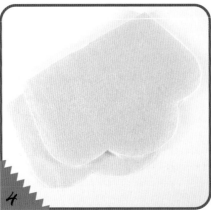

1 Fold your fabric in half and draw around the occasion bag template outline on the fold as indicated.

2 Cut two pieces from outer fabric and two from lining. Fuse fleece onto the wrong sides of the outer fabrics.

3 Cut two side panels from outer fabric and two from lining; fuse fleece onto the wrong sides of the outer pieces.

4 Place your template on the fold of the fabric again and draw around the scalloped flap. Cut two from lining fabric and fuse fleece onto the wrong side of one piece.

5 With the fabric on the fold, draw, then cut one base piece from outer fabric and one from lining. Fuse fleece onto the wrong side of the outer fabric.

If you're not too confident sewing buttonholes, add a magnetic snap fastener instead.

Tip

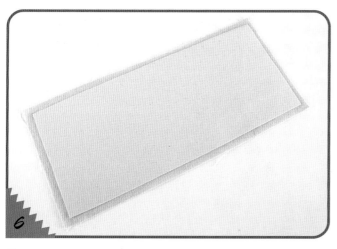

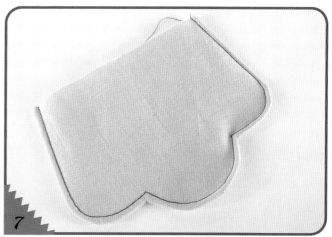

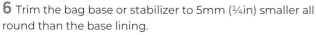

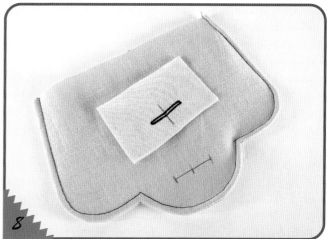

6 Trim the bag base or stabilizer to 5mm (¼in) smaller all round than the base lining.

7 Take the two flap pieces and sew right sides together, leaving the straight top side open. Trim the curves close to the seam, and snip into the 'V's in the seam allowance.

8 Turn right side out and press, then top-stitch around the curved edge. Mark the position of the buttonhole, centrally, 4cm (1½in) up from the bottom of the flap. I find it easier to stitch out a buttonhole on scrap fabric first, so that I can gauge the exact size and position. Sew the buttonhole and carefully cut through the middle with your quick unpick or a pair of small, sharp scissors.

9 Sew the two outer side panels to the front and back of the bag, right sides together, to make a tube. Sew in the bag base, then turn the right side out.

10 Cut two 7.5cm (3in) lengths of webbing. Thread each through a rectangular ring and tack/baste to the top of the side panels, facing inwards.

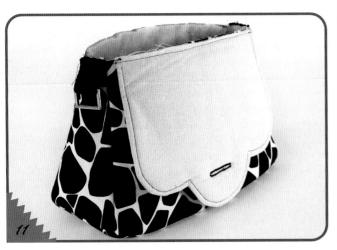

11 Tack/baste the flap, facing down and right sides together to the centre top of the back of the bag.

12 Sew the sides, front and back lining pieces right sides together, then add the lining base, but leave a turning gap of about 13cm (5in) in one seam. Drop the outer bag inside the lining with right sides together, then sew around the top. Adhere the bag base to the lining side of the bag.

13 When the glue is dry, turn right side out, then sew the opening closed.

14 Push the lining inside the bag and press, then top-stitch around the edge.

15 Fold over the flap and mark the position of the button. I add the button at this stage so that I know it's in exactly the right position. Sew on the button by hand, trying not to sew straight through to the lining.

16 Take the remaining webbing, thread back on itself through the centre of the slider and sew with a zigzag stitch.

17 Thread the end of the webbing through one of the rectangular rings on the side of your bag, then back through the slider.

18 Being careful not to twist the strap, take it through the opposite rectangular ring. Sew with a zigzag stitch to secure.

BOW CLUTCH

The bow fastening adds a feminine touch to this little clutch bag, which could easily be adapted to make a shoulder bag or wristlet if you prefer. I've used craft cotton for this bag, but you could try making it from satin or silk to turn it into a stunning evening or bridesmaid's bag!

You will need

- 66 x 51cm (26 x 20in) outer fabric for the bag and bow
- 102 x 46cm (40 x 18in) lining fabric, used also for flap
- 66 x 46cm (26 x 18in) fusible fleece
- 1 button

Finished size

28 x 20.5 x 5cm (11 x 8 x 2in)

Using your template

You will need to use the clutch bag outline from TEMPLATE 1, the round flap outline from TEMPLATE 1 and the wide strap outline from TEMPLATE 2. Place both templates on the fold of the fabric as indicated.

Template 1

Template 1

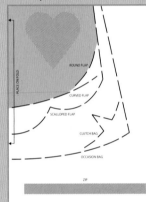

Template 2

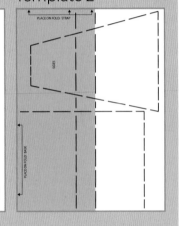

1 Fold your fabric in half, place the template over the fold where indicated, and draw around the clutch bag shape. Cut two pieces from outer fabric and two from your lining fabric, fuse fleece to the wrong side of the outer fabric.

To add a simple strap, sew the ends of a length of ribbon or cord, facing downwards, over the side seams of the outer bag before step 11.

Tip

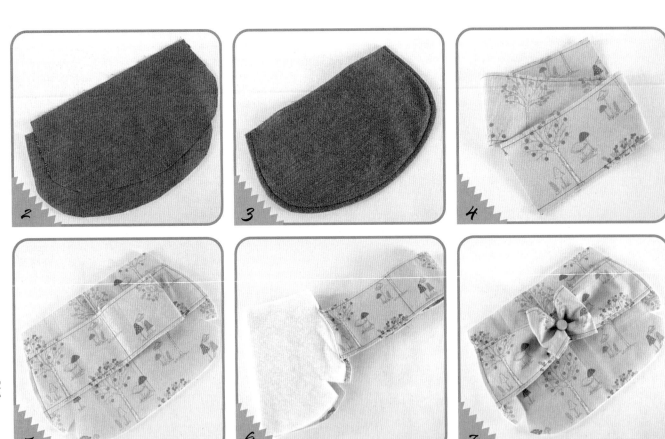

2 Cut out two round flap pieces from lining fabric, then fuse fleece to the wrong side of one piece.

3 Sew the two flap pieces right sides together, leaving the top straight edge open. Cut around the curve with pinking shears, turn right side out and press. Top-stitch around the seam.

4 To make the bow, cut two pieces of outer fabric from the wide strap template. Sew right sides together along the long sides, turn right side out and press. Top-stitch along the seams.

5 Place the bow across the front of the bag, 2.5cm (1in) from the top. Sew the sides of the strip to the edge of the bag, then trim the ends of the bow strip to the same shape as the bag. Fold the bag in half to mark the centre. Mark the point from each side of the bow where it sits over the centre line, so you have a fold of bow fabric.

6 Pull the bow away from the bag and, keeping it folded, sew along the marked line.

7 Open out the bag piece and the bow strip will sit neatly across the outer fabric. Press the folded section flat. Pinch the centre of the bow and hand-sew a couple of stitches, then add the button over the pleats. Don't gather the bow too tightly as it may pull the sides of the bag inwards.

8 Sew the flap right sides together, centrally, to the top of the back of the bag.

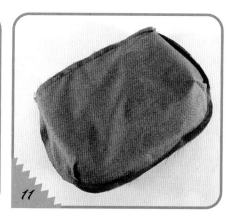

9 Sew the darts into the outer and lining pieces. Fold the cut-out 'V' shapes right sides together, then start sewing from the raw edges and slightly curve your stitch line to avoid the darts looking too pointy. Knot the inner ends of the thread to stop the stitches unravelling. Sew the two outer pieces right sides together, matching up the darts on each side, and leaving the top open. Snip around the curved seam with pinking shears, then turn right side out.

10 Sew the lining pieces right sides together in the same way, but this time leave a turning gap of about 10cm (4in) in the bottom seam.

11 Drop the outer bag into the lining so the right sides are together. Sew around the top.

12 Turn right side out and sew the opening closed.

13 Push the lining inside the bag and press. Top-stitch around the top of the bag, then fold the flap under the bow to fasten.

CURVED FLAP CLUTCH

As this cute little clutch bag has a loop ring on the side you could either use the wristlet or add a bag charm of your own, such as tassel, pompom or shop-bought option.

I've left the edge of my heart appliqué raw, as I think the look of the frayed edges works with my shabby-chic floral print fabric. Both the lining and outer fabrics are craft cottons. You don't have to use the heart, of course. You could try a star shape, for example, or personalize the bag with your initials.

Using your templates

You will need to use the clutch bag outline from TEMPLATE 1, the curved flap outline from TEMPLATE 1, the heart outline from TEMPLATE 1 and the wide strap outline from TEMPLATE 2. All the templates except the heart should be placed on the fold of the fabric as indicated.

If your main fabric has a large design, you could cut out a motif and appliqué it to the flap as for the handbag on page 34.

Tip

Template 1

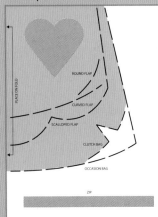

Template 1

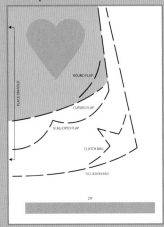

Template 1

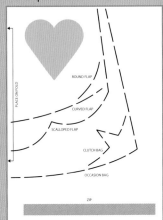

Template 2

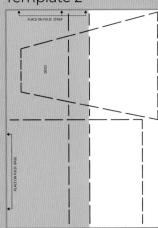

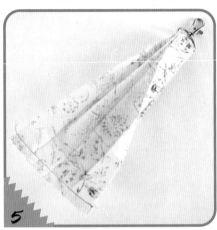

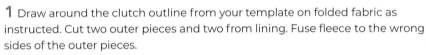

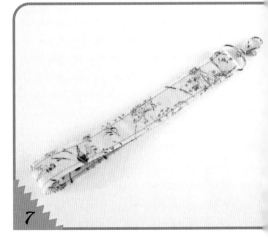

1 Draw around the clutch outline from your template on folded fabric as instructed. Cut two outer pieces and two from lining. Fuse fleece to the wrong sides of the outer pieces.

2 Cut two curved flap pieces from lining fabric, then fuse fleece to the wrong side of one piece. Cut out a heart shape from outer fabric, position to one side of the flap that is backed with fleece, then sew. Leave the edges raw and fray them a little if you wish.

3 Apply the thinner part of the magnetic snap fastener to the flap piece without fleece, centrally, 2.5cm (1in) up from the curved edge (see page 23). Sew the two flap pieces right sides together, leaving the top straight edge open. Snip around the curve with pinking shears, turn right side out and press. Top-stitch around the seam.

4 Cut out the wider strap from outer fabric. Fold in half lengthways and press, then fold the two long sides to the centre and press again. Fold the whole strap in half lengthways and press. Cut a 7.5cm (3in) length from one end. Top-stitch along the edges of this small piece, thread through the triangle loop ring and tack/baste the ends together.

5 Thread the remaining strap fabric through the swivel clasp, open out the fabric and sew the ends right sides together.

6 Re-fold the strap into the pressed creases, then top-stitch around both edges. You may find this easier using the free arm on your sewing machine.

7 Fold the strap flat with the seam inside the loop of the clasp, then sew across the strap, close to the loop.

8 Sew in the darts on the outer and lining fabric pieces. Fold the cut-out 'V' shapes right sides together, then start sewing from the raw edges and slightly curve your stitch line to avoid the darts looking too pointy. Knot the inner ends of the thread to stop the stitches unravelling. Tack/baste the triangle loop to the side of the front outer piece, facing inwards, 2cm (¾in) from the top.

9 Tack/baste the flap right sides together to the centre top of the back of the bag.

10 Sew the two outer pieces right sides together, leaving the top open. Snip around the curves with pinking shears; turn right side out. Fold over the flap and mark the position of the second half of the magnetic snap fastener – measure this to make sure it's in the centre before fitting the clasp.

11 Sew the lining pieces right sides together, leaving the top open and a gap of about 10cm (4in) in the bottom for turning.

12 Drop the outer bag inside the lining so that the right sides are together and sew around the top.

13 Turn right side out, then sew the opening closed.

14 Push the lining inside the bag, press, then top-stitch around the top. Clip the strap onto the triangle ring.

SCALLOPED FLAP CLUTCH

For this bag I've chosen the scalloped flap, and used a magnetic snap fastener to give the bag a bit of security. If preferred, you could use a button as on the handbag on page 38 or add a purely decorative button (see page 85).

My mustard-coloured outer fabric is a loose-weave linen, which I've backed with fusible fleece to give it stability. The floral lining and flap are quilting cotton. Bear in mind that a zipped or patch pocket can easily be added to the lining (see pages 20–21).

You will need

- 66 x 38cm (26 x 15in) outer fabric for the bag and strap
- 66 x 46cm (26 x 18in) lining fabric used, also for the flap
- 66 x 46cm (26 x 18in) fusible fleece
- Magnetic snap fastener

Finished size

28 x 20.5 x 5cm (11 x 8 x 2in)

Using your templates

You will need to use the clutch bag outline from TEMPLATE 1, the scalloped flap outline from TEMPLATE 1 and the wide strap outline from TEMPLATE 2. Place all the templates on the fold of the fabric, as indicated.

Template 1

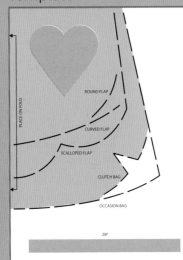

Template 1

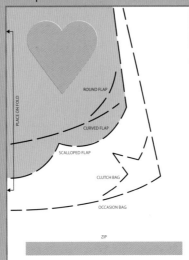

Template 2

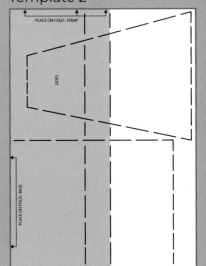

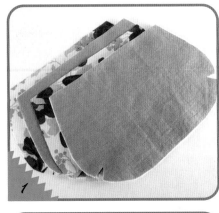

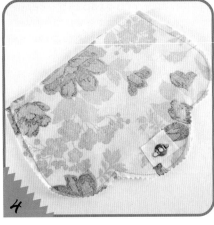

1 Fold your fabric in half, place the template over the fold where indicated, and draw around the clutch bag shape. Cut two pieces from outer fabric and two from lining fabric. Fuse fleece to the wrong side of the outer fabric.

2 With your fabric folded in half, draw around the scalloped flap; cut two from contrast flap fabric. Fuse fleece to the wrong side of one piece.

3 Take the flap fabric without the fleece and crease to mark the centre. Attach the slim half of your magnetic snap fastener 2.5cm (1in) up from the bottom (see page 23).

4 Sew the two flap pieces right sides together, leaving the straight top side open. Snip into the 'V' shapes and around the curved edges with pinking shears.

5 Turn right side out and press. Top-stitch around the seam.

6 Sew the darts into the outer and lining bag sections. Fold the cut-out 'V' shapes right sides together, then start sewing from the raw edges and slightly curve your stitch line to avoid the darts looking too pointy. Knot the inner ends of the thread to stop the stitches unravelling.

7 Fix the second part of the magnetic snap fastener centrally to the front of the bag, 11.5cm (4½in) down from the top.

8 Sew the front and back outer pieces right sides together, leaving the top edge open and making sure you match the darts on each side. Clip around the curves with pinking shears, then turn right side out.

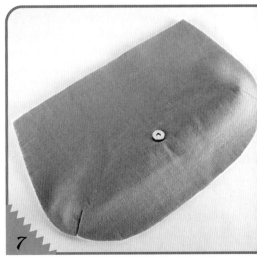

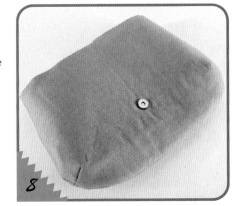

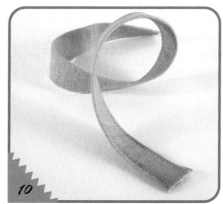

9 Pin the top of the flap to the centre back of the bag, right sides together, and tack/baste across the top. Remove the pins.

10 Make up the wider open-ended strap (see page 19). Cut it to a size that you will be able to fit your hand through. Mine is 41cm (16in) long.

11 Fold the strap in half, then tack/baste, facing downwards, over one side seam of the bag.

12 Sew the two lining pieces right sides together, leaving the straight top side open. Leave a turning gap of about 10cm (4in) in the base.

13 Drop the outer bag inside the lining so that the right sides are together, with the flap and strap tucked inside, then sew around the top edge. You'll find it easier to use the free arm on your sewing machine. Turn right side out through the turning gap.

14 Sew the opening closed. Then push the lining inside the bag and press. Use the free arm on your machine to help top-stitch around the top edge. Fold over the flap and you're ready to go!

ZIP CLUTCH

Adding a zip instead of a flap to this bag turns it into a cosmetic purse or wash bag, plus it's quite simple to add a wristlet if you wish, following the instructions for the Curved Flap Clutch on pages 48–51.

For a wash bag, choose a waterproof fabric for the lining and, if you wish, you can use a laminated fabric, oilcloth or faux-leather fabric for the outer.

You will need

- 66 x 23cm (26 x 9in) outer fabric
- 66 x 23cm (26 x 9in) lining fabric
- 66 x 23cm (26 x 9in) fusible fleece
- 30.5cm (12in) zip

Finished size
28 x 20.5 x 5cm (11 x 8 x 2in)

Using your template
You will need to use the clutch bag outline from TEMPLATE 1; place on the fold of the fabric as indicated.

Template 1

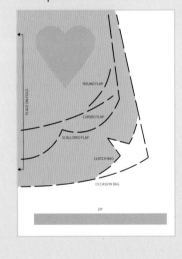

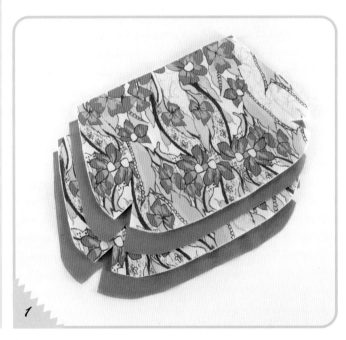

1 Cut out two outer and two lining pieces using the clutch template placed on the fold of the fabrics. Fuse fleece to the wrong sides of the outer pieces.

2 Sew in the darts for all four pieces. Fold the cut-out 'V' shapes right sides together, then start sewing from the raw edges and slightly curve your stitch line to avoid the darts looking too pointy. Knot the inner ends of the thread to stop the stitches unravelling.

3 Cut the ends of the zip, making it 20.5cm (8in) in length. Hand-sew the open end of the zip together, as this makes it easier to sew into the bag.

4 The zip should be shorter than the top of the bag, as shown.

5 Cut four pieces of outer fabric measuring 4cm (1½in) square. Place two pieces right sides together, with the end of the zip in the centre with all three edges meeting. Sew across the end of the fabric, trapping the zip in the middle, then turn the fabric back on itself and crease. Repeat with the opposite end of the zip, creating a fabric 'tab' on each end of the zip.

6 Pin, then sew the zip, facing downwards, over the top right side of one outer piece of fabric. Remove the pins.

7 Sew the top of the second outer side of the bag to the opposite side of the zip. Trim away any excess tab fabric.

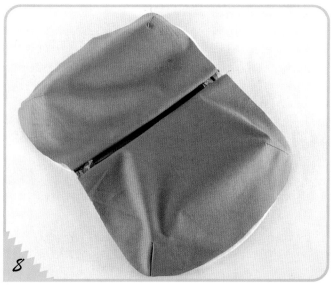

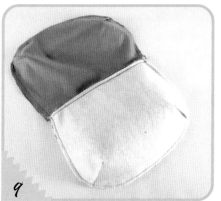

Use laminated lining fabric for a wipe-clean wash bag!

Tip

8 Sew the lining pieces to the zip, sandwiching the zip in between the outer and lining pieces.

9 Fold the bag pieces so that the outer and lining pieces lie right sides together, then sew all the way round, leaving a turning gap in the base of the lining of about 10cm (4in). When you approach the zip tabs, push them towards the lining.

10 Turn right side out, then sew the opening closed.

11 Push the lining inside the bag and press to finish.

COSMETIC BAG

Need a quick handmade gift for someone? This little pouch would be perfect for filling with make-up or crayons! I've used a printed linen with a cotton lining, but canvas or denim would create a modern look, and laminates would be perfect for a wipe-clean bag.

I like to use zips that are too long and cut them to size, as this means that I can move the slider out of the way of my stitching, plus, taking off the metal stoppers on the ends of the zip gives the bag a neater look. Don't do this if you're dressmaking though!

You will need

- 25.5 x 56cm (10 x 22in) outer fabric
- 25.5 x 56cm (10 x 22in) lining fabric
- 25.5 x 56cm (10 x 22in) fusible fleece
- 25.5cm (10in) zip
- 15cm (6in) of 5mm (¼in) wide ribbon (optional)

Finished size

28 x 20.5 x 6.5cm (11 x 8 x 2½in)

Using your template

You will need to use the occasion bag outline from TEMPLATE 1; place on the fold of the fabric as indicated.

Template 1

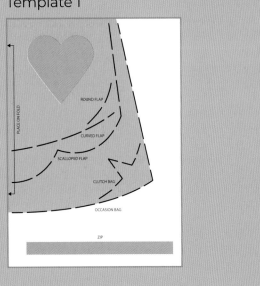

1 Using your occasion bag template on the fold of fabric, draw, then cut two outer pieces and two from lining. Fuse fleece to the wrong sides of the outer pieces.

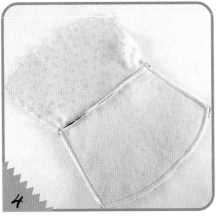

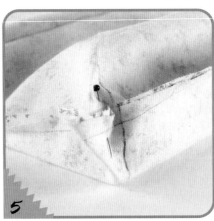

2 Cut off the ends of the zip and sew together the open end by hand. Place the zip face down over the top right side of one of the outer pieces and sew. You may find it useful to hold in place with a tacking/basting glue stick or stitches.

3 Sew the second outer piece to the opposite side of the zip. Trim off the excess zip.

4 Sew the top of the lining pieces right sides together to the other side of the zip tape. Fold the fabric so that the outer pieces and lining pieces are right sides together, then sew all the way around, leaving a turning gap of about 10cm (4in) in the base of the lining. As you approach the zip, push it towards the lining.

5 To make the base of the bag square, pinch the corners of the bag, so that the side seam sits over the base seam, and pin. Draw a line straight across each corner, 2.5cm (1in) from the point.

6 Sew across all four corners along these lines, removing any pins as you sew. Cut off the corners, then turn the bag right side out. Sew the opening closed.

7 Push the lining inside the bag and press, fold the ribbon in half and knot it through the pull on the end of your zip.

FRINGED HANDBAG

Take a trip back to the 1970s with this hippy-chic bag! It has two straps that can be knotted to make them the perfect length and to give a relaxed, stylish look. I've used a combination of silver faux leather and black linen-look fabric, which create a striking contrast, while the fringing is a shop-bought faux leather. Try using a tapestry-print canvas with an upholstery trim to create a colourful retro bag.

Using your templates

You will need to use the occasion bag outline from TEMPLATE 1, the curved flap template from TEMPLATE 1 and the wide strap outline from TEMPLATE 2. Place all the templates on the fold of the fabric, as indicated.

Template 1

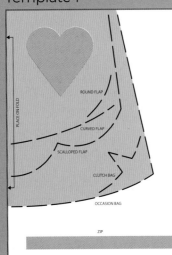

Template 1

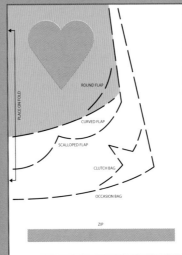

Template 2

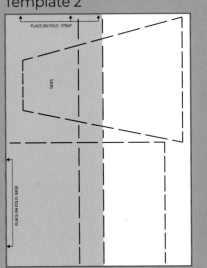

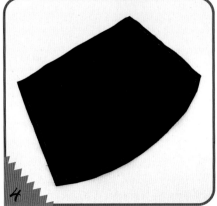

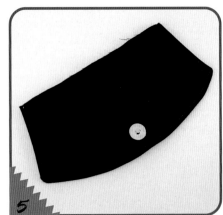

1 With the fabric on the fold, cut two faux leather and two lining pieces from the occasion bag template. Adhere fleece to the wrong side of the faux leather pieces with spray fabric adhesive (to avoid melting the fabric with your iron).

2 Sew the fringe to the bottom of the right side of one faux leather piece, facing inwards.

3 Sew the two faux leather pieces right sides together, leaving the top edge open. Make sure the fringing is tucked out of the way of the seam as you sew.

4 Sew the two lining pieces right sides together, leaving the top edge open and a turning gap in the base of about 13cm (5in).

5 With the fabric on the fold, cut out two curved flap pieces from lining fabric. Fuse fleece to the back of one piece. Apply the slim half of the magnetic snap fastener to the centre of the flap fabric without fleece, 2.5cm (1in) up from the curved edge. Sew the two pieces right sides together leaving the top edge open. Snip off the corners, turn right side out and press. Top-stitch around the curve.

6 Pin, then sew the flap, right sides together centrally to the back of the bag.

7 Remove any pins. Fold over the flap, mark the position, then fix the second half of the magnetic snap fastener to the front of the bag. Make up two straps using your template, each with one open and one closed end (see page 23). Sew the open ends to each side seam of the bag, facing downwards. Drop the outer bag inside the lining, right sides together, and sew around the top, being careful not to trap the ends of the straps or fringing. Turn right side out and sew the opening closed.

8 Push the lining inside the bag and press from the inside to avoid damaging the faux leather. Knot the two straps to the length you require. Groovy!

Make your own fringing by cutting a length of faux leather (or any fabric that doesn't fray) and snipping into it at 5mm (¼in) intervals.

Tip

PATCHWORK CLUTCH

This winning combination of patchworked squares and heart embroidery makes this pretty clutch bag a winner. I've deliberately sewn the strips of squares off-centre to give the bag a quirky look, but it also means I don't have to be too precise in matching corners! I used quilting cotton; pre-cut fabric strips would work perfectly.

You will need

- 6 strips of contrasting fabric, each measuring 96.5 x 6.25cm (38 x 2½in)
- 86.5 x 25.5cm (34 x 10in) lining fabric
- Erasable ink pen
- Free-motion foot for your sewing machine
- Magnetic snap fastener

Finished size

28 x 20.5 x 5cm (11 x 8 x 2in)

Using your templates

You will need to use the clutch bag outline from TEMPLATE 1, the round flap template from TEMPLATE 1 and the wide strap outline from TEMPLATE 2. Place all templates on the fold of the fabric when cutting out, as indicated.

Template 1

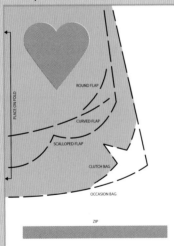

Template 1

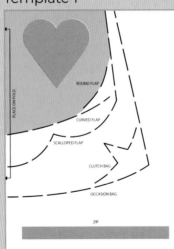

Template 2

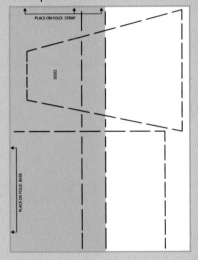

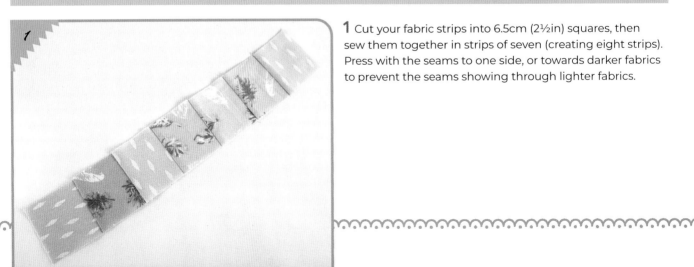

1 Cut your fabric strips into 6.5cm (2½in) squares, then sew them together in strips of seven (creating eight strips). Press with the seams to one side, or towards darker fabrics to prevent the seams showing through lighter fabrics.

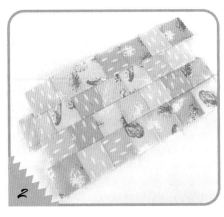

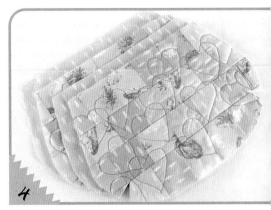

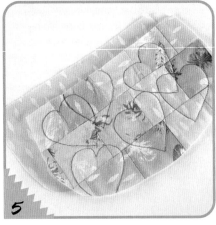

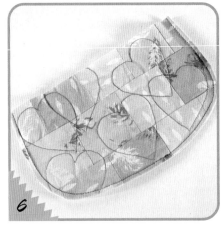

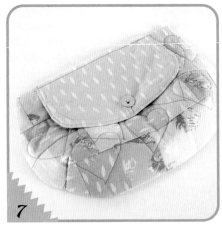

2 Sew these strips into two sets of four, offsetting the seams slightly as shown, then press again.

3 Fuse fleece to the wrong side of the patchworked pieces. Trace through the heart template randomly over the fabric, overlapping a few hearts as you go. Free-motion embroider over the outlines. Use a straight stitch on your sewing machine if you prefer.

4 Fold your patchwork pieces in half and place your clutch bag template over the top. Draw, then cut out two from patchworked fabric; cut two from lining fabric.

5 For the flap, sew together three strips of six squares, as in step 1. Fuse fleece to the wrong side and embroider hearts over the patchwork as in step 3. Using your template, cut out the round flap shape. Also cut one round flap from lining.

6 Apply the thinner part of the magnetic snap fastener to the flap lining, centrally, 2.5cm (1in) from the curved edge (see page 23). Sew the patchwork flap fabric and flap lining right sides together, leaving the top open. Turn right side out and press. Top-stitch around the curve.

7 Sew the darts into the outer and lining bag pieces. Fold the cut-out 'V' shapes right sides together, then start sewing from the raw edges and slightly curve your stitch line to avoid the darts looking too pointy. Knot the inner ends of the thread to stop the stitches unravelling. Tack/baste the flap right sides together to the top centre of the back of the bag.

8 To make the wristlet, sew together a strip of eight squares. Fold lengthways right sides together and sew to form a tube. Turn right side out and press, then top-stitch along the edges.

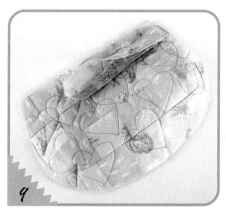

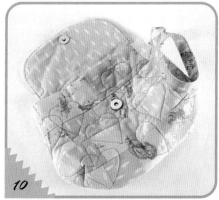

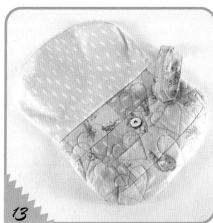

9 Fold the strap in half, and tack/baste it, facing inwards, to one side of the front of the bag, 2.5cm (1in) from the top.

10 Sew the front and back of the bag right sides together, leaving the top open. Turn right side out. Fold over the flap and mark the position of the second part of the magnetic snap fastener. Measure to make sure it's central, then fit the remaining part of the snap.

11 Sew the lining pieces right sides together, leaving the top open and a turning gap in the base of about 10cm (4in).

12 Drop the outer bag inside the lining, right sides together, and sew around the top.

13 Turn right side out, then sew the opening closed.

14 Push the lining inside the bag and press, then top-stitch around the top edge to finish.

PIPED HANDBAG

The piping on this patterned fabric gives the bag a crisp outline, while the lock adds a touch of class. The checked fabric I've used here is a poly-cotton dressmaking fabric that I've backed with fusible fleece to give the bag a little rigidity. I've also added a mesh bag base to accentuate the curve of the base.

You will need

- 91.5 x 56cm (36 x 22in) patterned outer fabric for the bag
- 91.5 x 76cm (36 x 30in) contrast plain fabric for the flap, piping, strap and lining
- 91.5 x 56cm (36 x 22in) fusible fleece or interfacing
- 127cm (50in) of 3mm (⅛in) piping cord
- Tongue clasp
- 11.5 x 29.25cm (4½ x 11½in) mesh bag base
- Wet fabric glue

Finished size

28 x 20.5 x 10cm (11 x 8 x 4in)

Using your templates

You will need to use the occasion bag outline from TEMPLATE 1, the curved flap from TEMPLATE 1, the wide strap outline from TEMPLATE 2, the side panel from TEMPLATE 2 and the bag base from TEMPLATE 2. All templates except the bag side should be placed on the fold of the fabric as indicated.

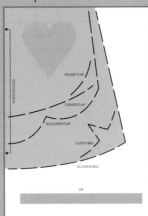

Template 1

Template 1

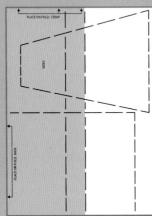

Template 2

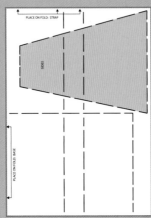

Template 2

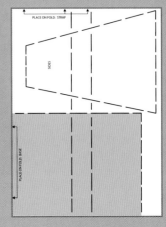

Template 2

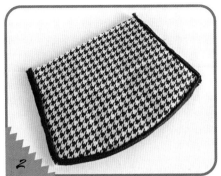

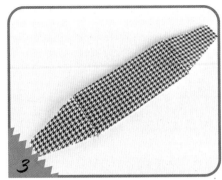

1 Cut 127cm (50in) of 4cm (1½in) wide plain fabric, and make up the piping following the instructions on page 22.

2 Fold your fabric in half, place the template over the fold and draw around the occasion bag shape. Cut two shapes from patterned (outer) fabric and two from plain (lining) fabric. Fuse fleece to the wrong sides of the patterned pieces. Sew the piping around the sides and bottom of each outer piece, with the raw edges together. Snip into the seam allowance of the piping as you approach the corners. Pull the piping out of the piping cord fabric by 5mm (¼in) at each end and snip.

3 Cut out two side pieces and one base piece from both patterned and plain fabrics. Fuse fleece to the wrong sides of the patterned fabric pieces. Sew the side panels of the patterned fabric pieces right sides together to the base.

4 Pin, then sew this long panel to the front of the bag.

5 Repeat with the remaining piece of patterned fabric. Turn right side out.

6 Make up the flap by folding your plain fabric and drawing around the curved flap template; cut two plain pieces of fabric and fuse fleece to the wrong side of one piece. Sew the two pieces right sides together leaving the straight top side open, then snip around the curve with pinking shears. Turn right side out and press, then top-stitch around the seam.

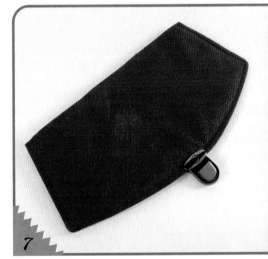

7 Measure and mark the centre of the curve and fix the tongue section of the clasp over the edge of the seam. This is usually held in place with two tiny screws on the back, but you can also secure with a dot of wet glue if you wish.

8 Tack/baste the flap right sides together centrally to the top of the back of the bag.

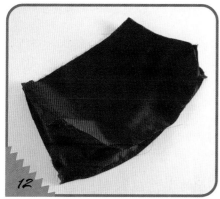

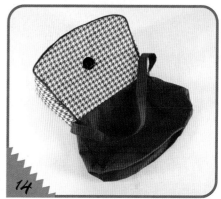

9 Fold the flap over to the front of the bag to mark the central position of the second part of the clasp, then fit it according to the manufacturer's instructions (these are usually secured with four prongs that are inserted through tiny incisions in the bag and pressed open).

10 Make up an open-ended strap following the instructions on page 19.

11 Tack/baste the strap, facing downwards, to each side of the top of the bag. Make sure the strap isn't twisted! Glue the mesh base into the bottom of the inside of the bag.

12 Sew together the lining front, back and sides, then insert the base, leaving a turning gap in one of the bottom seams of about 13cm (5in).

13 Drop the bag into the lining so that the right sides are together and the strap and flap are tucked inside, then sew around the top.

14 Turn right side out and sew the opening in the lining closed.

15 Push the lining inside the bag and top-stitch around the top edge to finish.

SLIM CLUTCH WITH SCALLOPED FLAP

For this bag, I've used the occasion bag template, but without the sides and base, making it a slim, elegant clutch, perfect for an evening out! I've chosen craft cotton for this bag: gingham for the outside and a stripe for the lining and flap. Notice how I've cut the heart appliqué on the bias of the gingham fabric, creating diamond shapes on the print that work well with the heart.

You will need

- 66 x 25.5cm (26 x 10in) outer fabric
- 66 x 46cm (26 x 18in) lining fabric
- 66 x 46cm (26 x 18in) fusible fleece
- Magnetic snap fastener

Finished size

28 x 20.5cm (11 x 8in)

Using your templates

You will need to use the occasion bag outline from TEMPLATE 1, the scalloped flap outline from TEMPLATE 1 and the heart outline from TEMPLATE 1. Place all templates except the heart on the fold of the fabric, as indicated.

Template 1

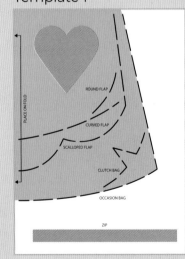

Template 1

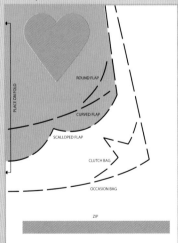

Template 1

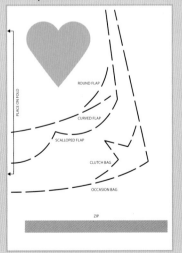

1 Cut out two outer and two lining pieces using the occasion bag template, then fuse fleece to the wrong sides of the outer pieces. Cut two scalloped flaps from lining fabric, then fuse fleece to the wrong side of one piece.

2 Cut a heart shape from your template. Position it in the centre of the fleeced side of the flap, 2.5cm (1in) up from the edge, then satin stitch all the way round. On the remaining flap fabric, apply the thinner half of the magnetic snap fastener centrally, 2.5cm (1in) from the bottom edge. Sew the two flap pieces right sides together, leaving the top open. Snip into the curves, then turn right side out and press. Top-stitch around the seam.

3 Sew the flap right sides together to the centre top of the back of the bag.

4 Sew the two outer pieces right sides together, leaving the top open. Snip off the corners and turn right side out. Fold the flap over and mark the position of the second part of the magnetic snap fastener. Check this is central before fitting the snap.

5 Sew the two lining pieces right sides together, leaving the top open and a turning gap in the base of about 10cm (4in).

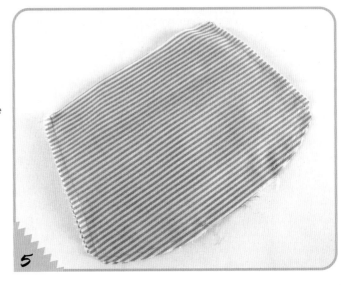

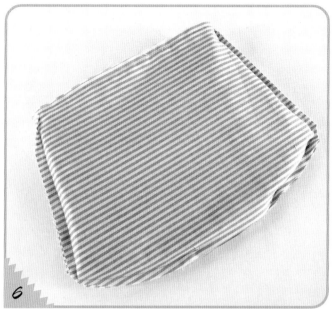

6 Drop the outer bag into the lining with right sides together and sew around the top.

7 Turn right side out and sew the opening closed.

8 Push the lining inside the bag and press, then top-stitch around the top edge to complete.

TRIPLE POCKET HANDBAG

This bag's three deep pockets are fantastic for keeping you organized! You basically get three bags in one. I've used a craft-weight cotton for this bag, with two plain pockets and one print; the linings are all patterned and I've used plain fabric for the flap.

Using your templates

You will need to use the occasion bag outline from TEMPLATE 1 and the curved flap outline from TEMPLATE 1. Place both templates on the fold of the fabric as indicated.

Template 1

Template 2

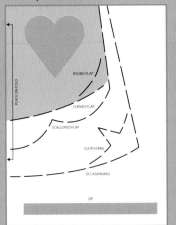

1 Using your occasion bag template on folded fabric as instructed, cut ten bag pattern pieces from patterned fabric, and two from plain fabric. Fuse fleece to the wrong sides of both plain pieces and four of the patterned pieces. The unfleeced patterned pieces will be used for the lining.

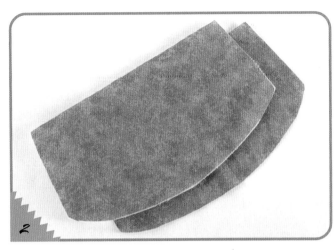

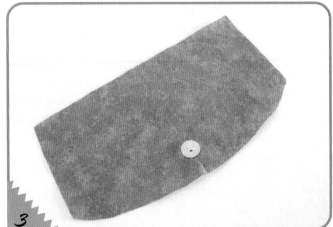

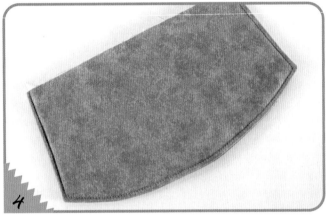

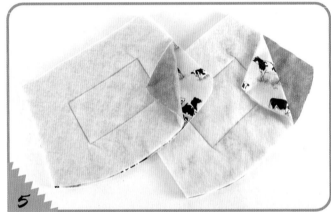

2 Cut two pieces of plain fabric using the curved flap template. Fuse fleece to the wrong side of one piece.

3 Apply the thin part of the magnetic snap fastener to the centre of the unfleeced fabric, 2.5cm (1in) up from the curved edge.

4 Sew the two flap pieces right sides together, leaving the top straight edge open. Turn right side out and press, then top-stitch around the seam.

5 Take the two plain pocket pieces and pin each one right sides together with a patterned piece. Draw a box in the centre of one side, 6.5cm (2½in) from each edge. Sew around these boxes, then remove the pins.

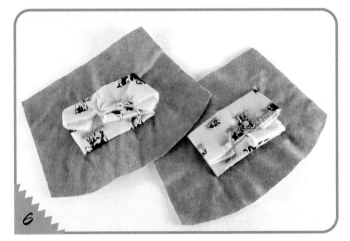

6 Fold the patterned fabric into the centre and pin.

7 Sew the two plain pieces right sides together, with the folded patterned fabric in the centre. Leave the top unsewn. Carefully turn right side out and remove the pins. Now fold the plain pocket and one of the patterned sides to the centre and pin as before.

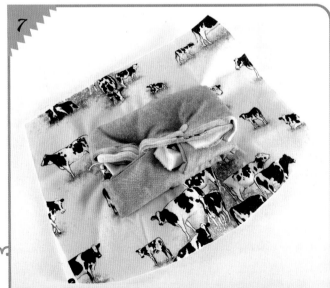

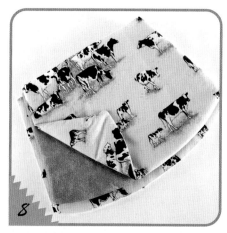

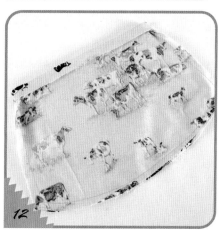

8 Place another patterned piece right side down over the top, and sew around the bottom three sides with the bulky fabric in the centre. Turn right side out, carefully removing any pins.

9 Fold the two pockets to the centre and pin.

10 Sew the flap right sides together to the centre top of the final patterned outer fabric piece, as shown.

11 Place this piece right side down over the folded pockets, and sew around the bottom three sides. Turn right side out and remove the pins. Now you have your three pockets! Fold over the flap, and mark the position of the second half of the magnetic snap fastener. Fix the snap centrally onto the front of the bag.

12 Sew together the lining pieces right sides together in pairs, leaving the top edges open. Fold the tops of the linings over by 1cm (½in) and press.

13 Drop the lining inside the front pocket and pin or clip the pocket and lining sections together. Top-stitch around the edge to secure the lining. Repeat this process for the back pocket (next to the flap).

14 To line the middle pocket, drop in the lining fabric, then place each end of the webbing strap over the side seams of the centre pocket, in between the outer and lining sections, before sewing. One final press and you're finished!

CHAIN STRAP CLUTCH

If you need an elegant evening bag, then look no further! The chain strap and brooch embellishment make this bag a classy accessory for any occasion. I've used craft cotton, and quilted the flap to add texture to the plain fabric.

You will need

- 66 x 25.5cm (26 x 10in) outer fabric
- 66 x 45cm (26 x 18in) lining fabric
- 66 x 45cm (26 x 18in) fusible fleece
- Magnetic snap fastener
- Large button or brooch
- Two 13mm (½in) D-rings
- Handbag chain with clips on each end

Finished size
28 x 20.5 x 5cm (11 x 8 x 2in)

Using your templates

You will need to use the clutch bag outline from TEMPLATE 1 and the scalloped flap outline from TEMPLATE 1. Place both templates on the fold of the fabric as indicated.

Template 1

Template 1

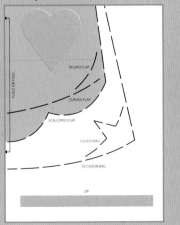

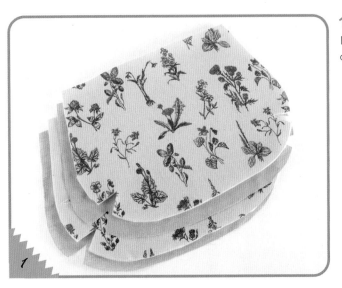

1 Use the clutch bag outline to cut two outer and two lining pieces, then fuse fleece to the wrong sides of the outer pieces.

2 Sew in the darts on all four pieces. Fold the cut-out 'V' shapes right sides together, then start sewing from the raw edges and slightly curve your stitch line to avoid the darts looking too pointy. Knot the inner ends of the thread to stop the stitches unravelling.

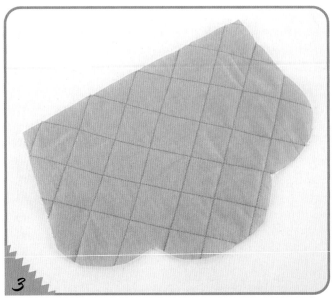

3 Cut two scalloped flap pieces from lining fabric, then fuse fleece to the wrong side of one piece. Draw diagonal lines 4cm (1½in) apart to form a grid with an erasable ink pen over the fleece-backed piece. Sew over these lines with a straight stitch to quilt.

4 On the remaining flap piece, fix one part of the magnetic snap fastener to the centre, 2.5cm (1in) up from the bottom curve.

5 Sew the two flap pieces right sides together, leaving the top edge open. Turn right side out and press. Top-stitch around the curved edges, then add your button or brooch to the front.

6 Sew the top of the flap right sides together centrally to the top of the back of the bag.

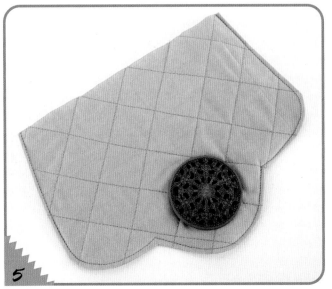

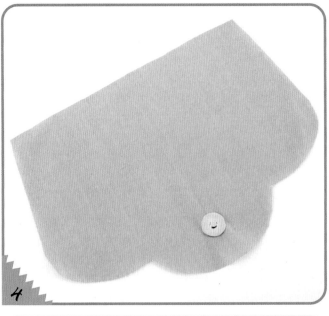

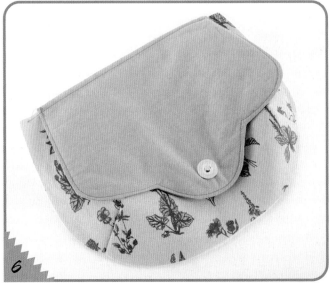

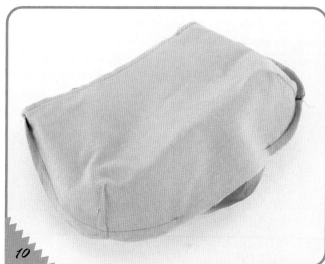

7 Sew the two outer bag pieces right sides together, leaving the top open. Turn right side out. Fold over the flap and mark the position of the second part of the magnetic snap fastener. Make sure your mark is in the centre of the bag, then fix the snap in place.

8 Cut two pieces of lining fabric measuring 5cm (2in) square. Fold two edges to the centre and crease, then fold in half to make a strip measuring 1cm (½in) wide. Top-stitch along both long sides. Thread each strip through a D-ring, fold over and secure with a dot of glue. It's helpful to hold the pieces with a fabric clip until dry.

9 Sew the D-ring tabs, facing downwards, over the side seams of the outer bag.

10 Sew the lining pieces right sides together, leaving the top open and a turning gap in the base of about 10cm (4in). Drop the outer bag inside the lining so that the right sides are together, then sew around the top edge.

11 Turn right side out, then sew the opening in the lining closed. Push the lining inside the bag and press, then top-stitch around the top edge. Clip the chain onto the D-rings and you're ready to go!

ZIPPED PURSE

This purse is a little unexpected as I used the occasion bag template, but upside down! Using the easiest method of fitting a zip, even a beginner can make a professional-looking, unusual purse. I've used a novelty craft cotton for my purse, but it would work just as well in a laminated fabric.

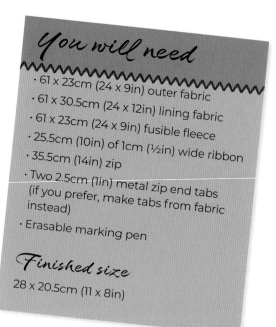

You will need

- 61 x 23cm (24 x 9in) outer fabric
- 61 x 30.5cm (24 x 12in) lining fabric
- 61 x 23cm (24 x 9in) fusible fleece
- 25.5cm (10in) of 1cm (½in) wide ribbon
- 35.5cm (14in) zip
- Two 2.5cm (1in) metal zip end tabs (if you prefer, make tabs from fabric instead)
- Erasable marking pen

Finished size
28 x 20.5cm (11 x 8in)

Using your template
You will need to use the occasion bag outline from TEMPLATE 1. Place on the fold of the fabric as indicated.

Template 1

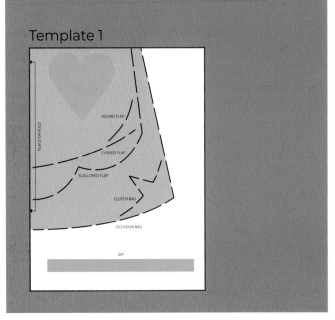

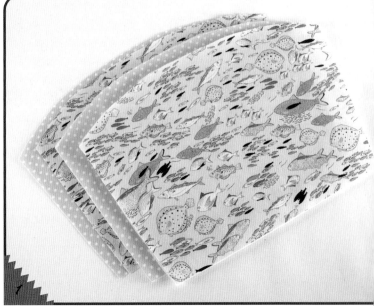

1 Turn your template upside down, place on the fold of the fabric and cut two outer and two lining pieces using the occasion bag outline. Fuse fleece onto the wrong side of the outer pieces.

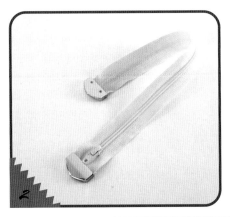

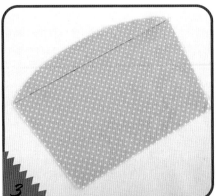

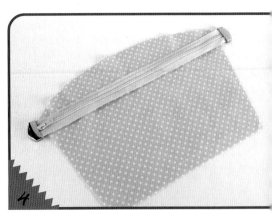

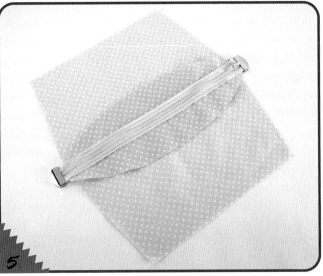

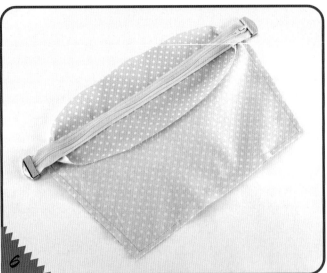

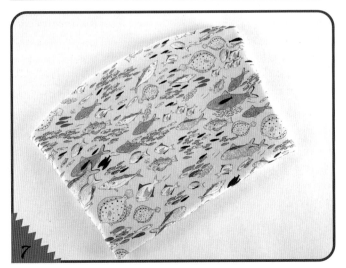

2 Cut off the ends of the zip, making it 30.5cm (12in) in length. Apply the zip end tabs according to the manufacturer's instructions (they usually have a couple of small screws to hold them in place).

3 Using your erasable ink pen, draw a line on the right side of each lining piece from one top corner to the other.

4 Place the zip, with the slider facing the top of the fabric, over the line. Use a tacking/basting glue stick or stitches to secure if you wish. Sew the zip in place, starting and stopping 5cm (2in) from each end of the zip.

5 Sew the opposite side of the zip to the remaining lining piece in the same way. Do not trim off the fabric seam allowance as you will need this.

6 Sew the sides and base of the lining pieces right sides together, leaving a turning gap in the bottom seam of about 10cm (4in).

7 Sew the outer pieces right sides together, leaving the top straight edge open. Turn right side out.

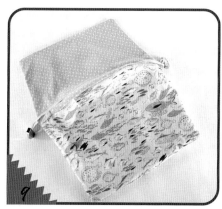

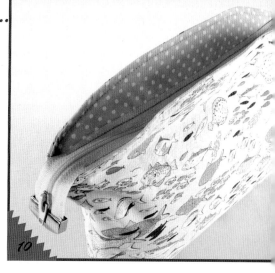

8 With the zip open, drop the outer bag inside the lining so that the right sides are together. Sew around the top of the purse.

9 Turn right side out and sew the opening in the lining closed.

10 Push the lining inside the bag, press, then top-stitch around the top edge.

11 Make up the flower from page 17 in lining fabric.

12 Cut the ribbon in half. Fold one piece in half and place under the flower to look like leaves, and sew to one side of the bag. Thread the remaining ribbon through the zip pull and knot.

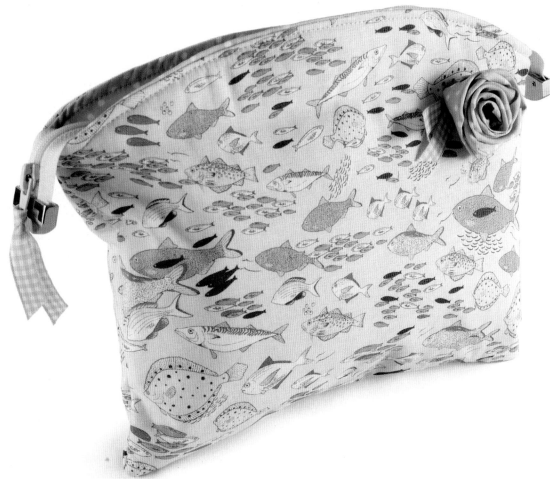

This stylish monochrome bag features a button closure and a webbing strap. The scalloped shape of the flap complements the pattern on the fabric. See pages 38–43.

This handbag's stylish clip-on handle gives it a shop-bought finish. If you don't want to use this kind of hardware, simply sew an open-ended handle into the side seams when making up. See pages 28–33 for instructions on making this bag.

A LITTLE EXTRA SOMETHING

This book shows how you can create lots of different bags using the same few templates. And by choosing alternative closures, straps and adornments you can add even more variation. The zipped purse on page 88 added another idea – using the bag template upside down. But why stop there? This little project offers yet another variation to tempt you.

MINI BRIEFCASE

To create the briefcase look, I've added a handle to the top of the bag and cut the bag back and flap as one piece. Make sure that if your fabric has a directional print, like mine, it is the right way up on the flap section.

You will need

- 63.5 x 25.5cm (25 x 10in) patterned outer fabric
- 63.5 x 35.5cm (25 x 14in) contrast plain fabric for the handle and lining
- 63.5 x 25.5cm (25 x 10in) fusible fleece or interfacing
- 2 buttons
- Tongue bag clasp

Finished size

28 x 20.5cm (11 x 8in)

Using your templates

You will need to use the occasion bag outline from TEMPLATE 1, the curved flap template from TEMPLATE 1 and the wide strap outline from TEMPLATE 2. Place the bag and flap templates on the fold of the fabric, as indicated.

Template 1

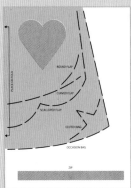

Template 1

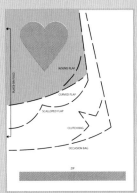

Template 2

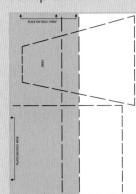

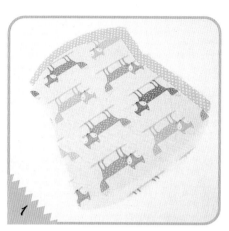

1

2

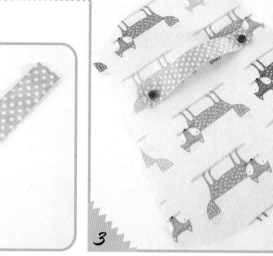

4

5

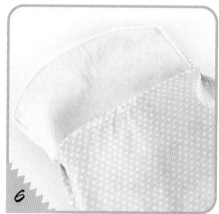

6

1 Place your template over folded outer fabric and draw around the occasion bag shape. Before cutting out, turn your template over so that the flap is on top of the bag, and draw around the curved flap, still on the fold. Cut out the shape; use this as a template to cut a piece from lining. Then use your occasion bag template to cut one front bag shape from outer fabric and one shape from lining. Fuse fleece to the wrong sides of the outer pieces.

2 Make up a closed-ended strap as on page 19, but this time, cut the fabric strip to 20.5cm (8in) in length rather than the full 25.5cm (10in) before you start.

3 Sew the handle to the right side of the outer bag piece, 2.5cm (1in) from either side, at the point where your flap would have met the top of the bag. Add a button to either side.

4 Add one half of the tongue clasp, according to the manufacturer's instructions, centrally, to the front of the bag, 10cm (4in) from the top of the bag.

5 Sew the outer bag back and front pieces right sides together, around the sides and bottom. Repeat with the lining pieces, this time leaving a turning gap of about 10cm (4in) in the bottom edge.

6 Drop the outer bag inside the lining, with the right sides together. Sew around the top: sew around the curve of the flap and around the top edge of the front of the bag. Snip into the corners and around the curve.

7 Turn right side out and press. Top-stitch around the bag front and flap.

8 Fit the second part of the tongue clasp to the centre front of the flap to finish.

7

INDEX

96

Join me in my sewing room!

I was so proud when my first book came out back in 2011. Then *Half Yard Heaven* appeared, selling over 100,000 copies, and since then I have been lucky enough to have written over 30 best-selling books published by Search Press, with more in the pipeline!

I've always wanted to feel close to my readers and to be able to help them on their sewing journey. In 2018 the lovely people at Search Press and I were discussing how I could inspire a new audience of sewers – that was the birth of the Half Yard Sewing Club. Five years later, the Club is bigger and better than ever. I've reached hundreds of thousands of dedicated sewers around the world on social media every year, many of whom have become members.

Joining the Club makes you part of our global sewing community, with exclusive monthly projects complete with downloadable patterns and helpful video instructions. You'll be able to print patterns out at home and start sewing them straight away! As well as monthly projects, you'll get access to the brilliant Half Yard project archive and a library of tips and techniques you can use at any time on your sewing journey. With exclusive offers, giveaways and discounts on books and materials, you'll soon recoup your subscription cost! What's more, you'll be able to join me on the members' forum and my free Facebook Lives and YouTube channels to ask me any questions you might have!

What do people love about the Club? Our wonderful member Reinette puts it better than I can when she says, 'the Half Yard Sewing Club offers so much more than just sewing tips and tutorials. We're all one happy family. And the price – it's absolutely value for money.' The Half Yard Sewing Club has brought together an amazing group of people from around the world, in a supportive and creative community where we share, learn from and teach each other, and have fun while we do it!

If you aren't a member yet, you can try the club for free with full access to all of my projects. I'm sure you'll love it and you are guaranteed a warm welcome from me and the other members! Just visit www.halfyardsewingclub.com/trial for the details.

See you soon!

When I think back to my childhood I remember sewing always being a huge part of it. My mum was a seamstress and had a sewing room with cupboards bursting with wonderful fabrics, old biscuit tins full of buttons and threads, and drawers crammed with ribbons and lace. I learnt the love of sewing and creativity from her, and I'm so delighted that my own daughter, Kimberley, is following in both our footsteps.

Debbie

Club favourites, Maddie and Robyn the rag dolls.

www.halfyardsewingclub.com

Half Yard™ Sewing Club

Half Yard Sewing Club
Reviews

www.halfyardsewingclub.com

Half Yard™
Sewing Club

> As a new member I am amazed at how much there is to pick and sew immediately. I want to do so many things! I love the informative tutorials and the easy, laid-back feel of the videos. Thank you for igniting my sewing passion again. – Sandra Phillips

> Now retired with grandchildren, I love the variety of projects, suitable for the children, myself and the home. All the instructions are so easy to follow. Seeing all the lovely projects and Member Makes spurs me on to be creative. – Heather Rodger

> The projects, video tutorials, tips and tricks are incredible value for money and the sense of community, although virtual, makes the club a really friendly place to be and to belong to. Debbie is an excellent tutor and there are so many projects that even beginner sewers could manage. My membership, which was a birthday gift, comes up for renewal in April and I will definitely be continuing my subscription! Love it. – Bonnie Wright

> I would recommend the HYSC to anyone for the following reasons:
> - Debbie shows and tells the members how to make each project in a very understandable way.
> - The projects are very varied, adaptable and always usable.
> - The "Tips", Members Makes and Ask a Member pages are most interesting and very useful.
> - In these days of higher prices, the HYSC is affordable. For the amount of knowledge you gain, it is great value.
> - Probably the nicest thing about the HYSC is the community of sewers it has gathered together from every corner of the world. It feels like a family who get along so well because of our shared love of sewing and the genuine care we have for each other.
> - Of course, the discount we receive from the "shop", is always a welcome perk.
>
> Thank you, Debbie, for sharing your wealth of knowledge with us members of the HYSC. – Geraldine Clifford